Understanding

Life

By

Kuhlula Ngobeni

Understanding Life

Written by

Kuhlula Ngobeni
Nkowa-Nkowa, Section D
House 296
Limpopo
South Africa

Telephone: 0607094391

Kuhlulangobeni57@gmail.com

Published by

William Jenkins
4036 Pine Street
Burnaby BC V5G 1Z5
Canada

williamhenryjenkins@gmail.com

editingservicesbilljenkins.ca

ISBN: 978-1-928164-56-2

Dedication

I dedicate this book to the churches and Christians and all kinds of leaders; and to the youth, their parents, our present generation and the generations to come.

Understanding Life

Acknowledgement

I would like to extend my sincere thanks to Krest Mashaba, Silver Nkomani, Golden Ngobeni, Thabang Mobosi and Fikile Mashaba.

Understanding Life

About The Author

Kuhlula Ngobeni

Kuhlula Ngobeni was born in June 1998. He lives in Nkowankowa Section D with his mother and twin brother and attends Bankuna Secondary School. Kuhlula has one sister named Ntwanano Ngobeni, one brother named Hitekani Ngobeni, and a twin brother named Hlulani Ngobeni.

He belongs to the Tabernacle of Praise and Grace Church and is a born-again person living for Christ.

He believes that his calling is to become an author. He started writing books in 2016, but did not realize that what he was writing was helping people. He knew that he loves helping people, so as people began telling him that he was helping them with his funny messages, they opened his eyes and showed him that writing books can help him reach the world. He wishes to help people spiritually and physically and decided to help people through writing books.

This book is intended to help all people, black and white, children and adults, men and women; to guide them on how to cope with life. The words in this book are real and are written about the reality of life, spiritually and physically.

Table of Contents

Understanding Life

Introduction

This is a motivational book guiding children and adults from all the struggles of life to reaching success and restoring humanity and the natural potential of humans. It helps in all the hard times in life.

It helps in the following aspects:

- educational struggle
- family struggle
- restoring human nature
- personal struggles

This is not a spiritual book, but I put God first in everything. If you can accept Him as your Lord and Saviour, I promise that you won't regret accepting Him. There's nothing that can be hard for you to do. See Philippians 4 verse 13 (KJV) *I can do all things through Christ which strengthens me.*

When God comes, He closes all the open gaps in our lives. He closed mine unexpectedly. We all hear how people call God with different names because He becomes many things and changes according to our desires.

I could not believe how he changed my life and removed the stress I had due to my thinking of parents. Psalm 27 says *"My father and mother may abandon me, but the Lord will take care of me."* The writer of the Psalm knew that God can become everything that a person wants in this world. My life has changed since I accepted Jesus in my life. He is a father to the fatherless and a mother to the motherless. He changed everything in my life. He can also change yours. Try accepting Him or always live in stress.

I know because although I don't have my parents, God replaced their space in my life. For God to change your life or to show you his power you don't have to do anything other than to accept him as your personal Saviour and believe that he can change your life. I was a lost sheep until someone came to advise me. Now it has changed.

I hope and wish you can quickly understand that God is the Creator of the uncreated. God is everything that any person can want in their lives. Life without parents is tough, but God is a parent to those who don't have parents.

Understanding Life

Understanding Life

Growing Up in Poverty

Some of us grew up in poverty, while others were living a good life.

When you are living in poverty you are surviving with very little money. This life is inferior in quality and usually you have to get along without many possessions.

What causes poverty? We tend to complain when we are facing or living in poverty. Poverty is not a curse. The decisions we make from a young age are the reasons some of us live in poverty. Many people are living in poverty simply because of the decisions they have made.

How can we fight poverty? One way is to go to school in order to get education. I know someone who grew in a poor family, but now he is a rich man and independent. Observing this man and his life and how successful he became was a motivation to me. I learned that you can fight poverty even though living in it and win by following your dreams and getting education.

Most people say education is a key to success, but I say education is a great weapon to fight poverty. It does not matter how poor you are. What matters is that you get education in order to get out of the poor background and say "Hello" to a new good life.

Poverty makes people think they are not worthy of living, but poverty is not a curse. It is the result of choices you or your family have made.

To get out of poverty, focus on your future. Make good decisions that will bring good results. Let the poverty punish you while you are still young and living in it, but prepare weapons to fight it. Know that a hard worker always receives good results and a good reward.

Understanding Life

There's one weapon that can defeat poverty and that weapon is the greatest weapon in the whole world. It is going to school, becoming educated, graduating, going to work and becoming independent.

Understanding Life

Understanding Life

To Accept is to Rest

I was raised in a poor family where I never saw my mother or my father. I was raised by my cousin who was one year older than I. It was her responsibility to take care of me as her young brother.

When my cousin died, I realized that I had nobody to take good care of me, so I started to ask myself many questions about life.

I used to cry day after day, both day and night. I did not even have time to concentrate at school because of how tough life was for me.

All my friends and neighbors were living a good life and eating a proper meal every day while I was starving. It was very painful and stressful for me. My friend was eating well and getting everything he wanted from his parents. I was stressing every day because I was asking myself questions such as "Why was I not born in that family?". I was asking myself questions about life.

My friend used to get everything he wanted, but I felt like a lost child with nothing in the world. I had nobody to ask for money or anything. I felt stressed until I went to church.

The first time I went to church, the Pastor was preaching about "Let not your heart be troubled." From that day on, I learned to accept what life gives and what it takes. I started to get rest after accepting everything that was happening in my life, because I understood that what happens to you in this life you don't choose, but life chooses for you. I also realized that everything has its own purpose and time to happen.

Moral Lesson

Sometimes in life we have to accept what has happened and move on with our life. You cannot change what has happened, but you can change what could happen next. Learning to accept is allowing you to grow. To accept is to understand that something that happened has happened and nothing can be done to change it.

We usually find it hard to accept that certain people are no longer present in our lives, without knowing why.

There's nothing that is harder than to accept that things which are happening in our lives are not under our control. Many times we find ourselves in stress, crying because we can't accept what we face.

One thing we must always know is that there are some things which we cannot change and do not want to accept, but to accept is a good choice to take. Learn to accept and move on.

Holding unto what has happened will not give you rest nor peace, but sorrow and pain. We usually find healing in our hearts after we have accepted what happens and learn to move on. You cannot move on while still holding unto what happened. Learn to accept what life brings and what life takes and you will live a peaceful life.

Understanding Life

Understanding Life

Stop Holding Onto the Past

The past is the previous time that indicates how long ago something has happened. For many people, the past rules the present and hinders the future. Many people are hindering their future because of holding on to the past. Holding unto the past is like living in the past and prevents you from be able to live in the present or the future.

Many times we don't look at what will come in our life when we hold unto the past, but we think it will help us to remember to take revenge on people who wronged us. We hold the past for many reasons that may end up making us make poor decisions.

The idea of holding the past in order to pay revenge is wrong because it hinders our life and the forward movement of it. The more you hold onto the past, the more you close the door to the future and the more you complicate the present. Let go of the past and let in the present and the future.

The past makes us who we are today, not who we were. Run towards your goals; never run to satisfy things of the past. The past, the present and the future don't match and are not one thing. They follow each other, but don't walk together. Stay strong in life by letting go of the past.

Understanding Life

You Can Be Whomever You Wish To Be

As long as you breathe, you have life. Whether you are a cripple, blind, deaf or mute, whether you use a machine to eat food, to drink, to go to the toilet, to speak, to move or to hear, even if more things are happening in your life, the important thing is that you can breathe. Breathing means that you have life. As long as you breathe you are equal to any human being on earth. It does not matter how people treat you or what they say about you or about who you are or what you are.

You can be mentally disturbed or mentally well. The point is that we are all humans and we are all one unto the Creator who created us in his own image.

Some people are born without certain parts or with disturbances in their bodies. While growing up they realize they can't walk, speak, hear, or have some other disability. They may believe that they can't become who they want to be in life and think that God has created them to be useless unto the world, but God has a purpose why he created each of us, regardless of the condition you find yourself in.

Thinking that you are useless is a mistake. You can do almost anything as long as you breathe.

Never be discouraged by what you see in other people's lives. Never be discouraged by what people say about you. I want you to know that you are born for a purpose and God has good plans for your life. God plans not to harm you, but to give you hope and a good future. Don't think that God is wrong for creating you as He has. God does things with a reason. He has plans for the cripple, for the blind, for all kinds of people.

I know one young man who was born without legs and hands, but he can do anything that he wants to do and

15

be who he wants to be. He can do things that others who have both hands and legs are not able to do.

As long as you are living, you are a precious creature, a wonderfully created creature. You are an awesome image of God. Remember, in the beginning God said let us make man in our own image, then he created Adam and Eve. We are the descendants of Abraham and are God's creations. In everything, no matter how we see ourselves, we are God's image. We are like God.

Never care about your body, but care about yourself; you are not your body, you are yourself. Can your blindness stop you from getting to your destiny? Can anything stop you? If there were nothing to stop you from being born, there is nothing that can stop you from reaching your destination. You can be whomever you want to be as long as you don't allow what you lack to stop you. Can I stop you? Can anybody stop you? If not, then don't stop yourself.

There's your body and there's the real you. Use anything you have to go to your destiny. Stop worrying about what you don't have. You can make it! You are powerful and you are a human who has sufficient ability.

Understanding Life

Understanding Life

You Need a Destiny Helper

We all need destiny helpers to make it to our destination.

A destiny helper is someone who encourages you and supports you. A destiny helper is someone who believes in you, in your dreams and vision, and who is willing to help you reach to your destiny.

A destiny helper is a person encouraged and empowered by God to help you reach your destiny.

You need a destiny helper because sometimes in life we can't stand alone without someone supporting us. When we face hardships, sometimes we end up giving up on our dreams. That's why we need a destiny helper. You can't fulfil your destiny without someone helping you.

There is a man described in the Bible in the book of Exodus Chapter 14 named Moses. Moses could not fulfil his destiny by himself. He needed a destiny helper and God raised Aaron for him and it was through the help of Aaron that he was able to deliver the children of Israel out of bondage.

We need a destiny helper. Moses could not fulfil a destiny alone, but God raised Aaron for him. God has raised someone for you, someone to help you fulfil your destiny. There is a saying that two are better than one. It means that with two or more people you are more likely to be able to bring about a change.

Destiny is not about one person making it in life, but about an agreement among two or more people to fulfil a destiny. Every person on earth reaches that time where they get tired and need another person's recommendation to survive what they are going through. There are times where you need some advice.

It does not matter how a person helps you. As long as a person comes to speak with you when you are facing a challenge, that person is helping you. Even when that person does not talk about what you are facing, he or she is helping you to avoid stress about your problems by yourself. It helps a lot when a person comes to speak with you about the things you are going through. While the person talking to you may not know that he is helping you, you realize that he is counselling you in your problems.

Many people get recommendations from friends, siblings, peers or family members, but they end up saying no nobody helped me to do this. The fact is that if nobody had come to assist you, you would not be free from your problems now.

Every person, black or white, great or small, faces difficult times and we all want to make it to our destination in life. We need one another to survive in this world. Many times we don't see it when people help us, but the fact is that people are always helping us without first alerting us that they want to help.

How do I know my destiny helpers?

- They advise us.
- They build our faith.
- They give us hope.
- They don't discourage us.
- They don't judge us.
- They care much.
- They help us overcome our problems.

Why people miss their destiny helpers

Sometimes we pray unto the Lord asking Him to send us destiny helpers, but we end up missing them. Sometimes we seek them, but when they come we don't recognize them and we end up missing them. Rev. Lucy Natasha once said

"Be kind to everyone you meet; treat everybody with kindness because you don't know who is your destiny helper." Kindness is the language that the blind see and the deaf hear.

We miss our destiny helpers because of arrogance without kindness. Be kind to everyone you meet.

Understanding Life

Making a Mistake

Life can be painful and confusing to everyone in the world. If we want to know how life is evil check here. In the Bible it says that Paul was killing many people, not because he wanted to do that, but because he was controlled by his heart which was filled with evil. As the truth arrived in him in the form of Jesus, his life changed from bad to good.

Many people in the world are busy doing what they don't want to do because of a lot of things they go through. Some of the bad things that make women start selling their bodies or men start to be thieves are because of pressure. Women who sell their bodies end up being called by names like prostitute, drunkard or thief, but all these people didn't know that they would be called by these names. Because they have found nobody to care for them when they are in need, they started to do a lot of things until evilness filled their hearts. Many people are criminals, prostitutes and thieves because of poverty.

No matter what people can call you or how they treat you, as long as you know from your heart that the bad things you did were not from your heart, there will be a way to better your life again. If you change, some will believe that you have changed and appreciate it, but some will not believe even to appreciate it. Even when they don't believe you, don't go back to doing bad things. To the wise it is known that a change of a person from bad to good or from evil to good does not take a year, a month or a day, but it takes the present moment. By deciding that you are changing, from your mind you are a changed person. When you begin to bring out the fruits of your words as you said you are changing, then we find conclusion of your change.

Many people have changed from bad works to good works, but because some people don't believe they have changed, then they again go back to bad works because they were never appreciated. They were doubted when they tried. Never be discouraged by people. Always know that the world will always have those who will appreciate the good works and those who don't appreciate the good works. Some people will say "No, no, that person cannot change. He or she has been doing evil for decades." Let me remind you that everything has its own time. Such people who say those words are the ones who don't appreciate the change of things in the world.

To decide to change from bad activities to good activities is a good decision even when people don't appreciate your change. Don't go back to do evil because of those who doubt your change, but keep on moving to a good future. One day you will see the benefits of your changing and those people that did not appreciate your change will praise God when they begin to see your benefits; they will congratulate you for changing. Keep on moving on your mind decision. Change is a good thing to do. Everyone makes mistakes which affect other people badly.

While you love someone a lot, your parents, friends or husband or wife, you may make a mistake that affects them; however, your mistake should not be defining you. A person can be fooled by his friends and drink alcohol, but that does not make that person a drunkard. It does not matter what kind of love you have for another person, even if you can promise to be faithful, you will make some mistakes. When a person you trust makes a mistake, that does not mean unfaithfulness. Every person in the whole world makes his or her own mistakes. Everyone is unique; as we are not the same, we will not make the same mistakes.

Always you must know that there are things which you will not hide from as long as you are living in this world. These include:

- sadness

- agony

- joy

- anger

- change of mood

- laziness

- pain

- tears

All the things mentioned above are the things that a person who loves you can do to you. Every person goes through those feelings even when you are rich or poor, young or old, black or white; we are all the same and created from the same image of God. In most places people are being judged by their mistakes. A mistake does not reflect a person behaviour or nature. People do make mistakes because they were misled by something.

If you know that you make mistakes, then you must also know that even others make mistakes. The fact is that same mistake can't be done twice or more, but a mistake can be done once and not be repeated. A person will always make mistakes until death arrives. It does not matter how old you are, young or old, you have children or you don't have, you will make mistakes because you are a human. Nobody is perfect in life. There are lot of mistakes a person can make.

Causes of mistakes

- smoking

- alcohol

- peer pressure

- lack of knowledge

- anger

- revenge
- Without first thinking of the outcome

Kinds of mistakes

- Lying
- Killing
- Fornicating
- Getting drunk
- Being late for an important event
- Breaking a relationship
- Forgetting important things
- Fighting
- Insulting

There are lot of mistakes that can be forgiven, but some cannot be erased once they are made. The fact is that if someone has done something that cannot be erased, it does not mean he can't be forgiven and it does not mean he did it on purpose. We need to forgive and try to forget. Holding the past won't help us. Let it go.

The Darkness

Sometimes life is good; sometimes it's bad and ugly. That's how it is with everything on earth.

I grew up with my uncle and step-dad without having my own parents not even knowing the names of my parents. I never had anyone talking about my parents or mentioning their names. There's nothing that I know about my parents, but it's better that at last I know their faces from the pictures of my late uncle.

My mother was a teacher before she died. As a teacher, she used to go with me when she went around teaching what she used to teach. She used to make lot of things such as drawings and design. She was carrying books on her head and she would put me on her back as I was a child. My father would do the same, carrying books on his head and putting my sister at his back. A time came when my mother died and my father was moved to stay far from us.

As my father moved to stay far away, life became tough. In the beginning everything started falling apart. After a month my father also died. Life started being darker than in the previous according to what my Godfather told me. I was staying with my sister and my next door friend. There became a time when I didn't even know where to sleep because I had no room, and I did not know what to eat because I had no family. I was living with my sister and the next door child.

As this time of lacking began, sometimes I would sleep without eating and I would sleep on the floor. The funny part is that I reached 26 years without having a bed, a blanket, or a room. I was staying with rich friends and sometimes I would go into their rooms and wish I was raised in that family of my friends.

Sometimes I would wish to be adopted by another family. Sometimes when I was hungry, I would eat porridge alone without anything to eat with. In my heart I would say this will end and indeed it will all end, for nothing lasts forever; everything passes.

There are a lot of people facing this. Some kill themselves, but I learned to accept everything that came my way. Stressing won't change anything, but accepting can change lot of things. Stay strong! You won't die like that; what you are going through now will all pass. No matter how people treat you, whether they laugh or don't laugh, nothing will last forever. Everything changes. Wait for the right time and you will see the change.

The Hurting Change of Life

As we live in life, we start seeing lot of good and bad things which were hidden because of our age. I came across tough and gigantic changes of life where I found out that everyone in the world stands for himself or herself in order to get a good future.

When I was about 12 to 14 years of age, I wanted to grow fast so I could have all my future desires. As a young boy, I was wishing to have a good family with good properties such as cars, a big house and lot of money, but in all this I never had time to think about the steps required to get all those luxurious things and a good wife.

All I wanted was a good life, but now I know that there are steps I need to take to reach a career. I am starting to realize how tough life is. The more I grow, it seems that the challenges of life increase more.

When I was young, I used to get everything I wanted even though I was not living with my parents, but as the years increased, all those people who used to give me things were scattered away and I was left alone in my own world.

I tried to ask for money from my step-mom; she gave me nothing. I tried to write a letter to my dad asking for a direction in everything of life. I did not get even one instruction. I felt like the world was swallowing me horribly.

Never think that people will support you every day until you die. You have to wake up from your sleep and open your eyes. There are a lot of things which can tempt a person when he is young, such as, for example, when your family buys you something, perhaps a car. You will think that they will always buy things for you until you die, and that thought is a tempting one. That won't happen in your lifetime.

Another temptation is that when you see everyone caring too much for you, even the community, you will be tempted to think it will last forever. As time moves on, you will find out that a lot of things which people used to do are no longer happening. When you face a lot of unexpected changes, you will find out that your community will not do anything for you because they expect you to do the things that they used to do for you.

Because of the mentality of childhood, when these changes happened I was so hurt because I never knew that things changed this way. There are many tempting thoughts coming from people's actions. Here is a reminder: always prepare for your future because it is in your hands. In a short time you will be expected to provide for yourself. If the tempting thoughts can overcome you, you will find yourself in a big danger where you depend on people for everything.

Many people are being tempted by what their parents have and how they are treated by the community and family, but they forget that what their parents have is not for them. They also do not appreciate that their parents won't live forever. Parents die; everyone dies, for nothing physical lasts forever. There's only one thing that lasts forever in the whole world and that is the Word of God. All the creations die and pass .Things expire.

Wake up from the sleep and start preparing for your future, because of all that other people have, none of it is yours. Wake up and make a better life for yourself. You are in your own world and on your own ground when you are 18 years old. The ball is in your court; play it, play it, play it. Play it for your own good and your future. You can do anything you want to do; use anything you have in you. You can do it; you have the ability; you are powerful.

Understanding Life

Understanding Life

Education Gives Good Life

Education is the process or art of imparting knowledge, skill and judgment. It gives skills, facts and ideas that have been learned neither formally or informally. It provides a good life for many people. It can be described as a 70 percent good life giver. About 30 percent are the ones who get a good life through the help of God and the help of the Devil. Every person is expected to go to school to be educated because there are many things to be learned that make our lives easy.

The knowledge or information that we get from school is what is needed to let us have a good life. It also teaches us to cope with life and how to respond to life when winds come to harm us. Not everyone benefits from formal education. Some people have great manual skills, but find it hard to understand concepts.

That does not mean you should not go to school. Education is important in our everyday life. The fact is that not all of us will prosper in education. Some will fail until they drop out and even that is better than staying at home without first trying to find out how you respond to education. Do not drop out of school until you see what talents God has given you.

Keep on studying hard even when you fail. Tell the teachers about how you are responding to the teaching. They will try to recognise your gift and suggest where you should go to study where your gift can be fed with knowledge. Continue to study even when you are having difficulty in education for you still have to feed the gift that God has given you.

You might go and study at college or in university. To go and study is a must, even when you did not do well in school. Do not be too lazy to study hard, because you may lead yourself astray by saying education is not going to bring prosperity. Many people have done well without education, but it's not really their choice. It is how God's plan works according to the intelligence He gave to all people.

If you drop-out of school without discussing it with your elders at home or at school, you will face difficult problems. Dropping out of school is not a decision that you should take alone. No matter how badly you are failing at school, first tell your elders at home or school you are thinking of dropping out because you need these people to help you to move on with life. These people are the ones that have to help you to reach your dreams, but when you take a decision alone, they will say 'Help yourself because you think you are strong alone.'

Sometimes you will find that the people you started with from grade R to grade 9 are on top of you when you go to grade 10, even some who you thought would not be up with you. As you start to realize this, you may think that you are not good enough to continue in school. That is not true; you just have to study harder.

Remember this: being behind someone with brains is not a problem. We are not all given the same brains by God. Sometimes you will see a child younger than you, being smarter than you and passing more than you, while you are busy failing. What a person must do is to study harder and concentrate on reaching his or her own goal without comparing himself or herself with other people. It's impossible for two people to have the same intelligence; even twins don't have the same intelligence.

As a learner never compare yourself with other learners, but fight for your purpose which is to progress from one grade to another grade. Let that be your purpose. Never care about whether someone is more intelligent than you. As long as you always progress to the next grade, let that be sufficient to you. Be grateful for what you have and never be jealous. You are unique. Find your gift and your potential. Find what God gave you and fight to make use of it.

Many went to universities and colleges, but still did not get jobs and have finished studying. If you didn't get a job, search yourself to find your natural gift. Your gift can be drawing, acting, painting, building, dancing, making jokes, motivating, hair making or any natural gift. Search for it and use it to benefit yourself and others.

Not all people will prosper through education. Some are gifted in other things.

Who are you? What can you do to make a change in the world and to make yourself benefit financially? You must know that you are not like other people. Sit down in front of a mirror and study yourself. Get into your mind and study yourself. Think until you reach your innermost beliefs.

Avoid being led by mob psychology, because you might lose your potential while chasing other people's potential, dreams, and abilities.

Never look down on education for it holds your brighter future. It has a high percentage of making a person prosper in life. There's nothing that makes life easier than when you have gone to school and finished your studies.

Even when you have money and are rich, but not educated, there are lot of things which can limit your potential, such as, for example, giving a speech to people, knowing how to stand and talk before people.

There are many things which can limit you. If you have the opportunity to go to school, use that opportunity to go and be educated.

Understanding Life

Time Management

Time is measured in seconds, minutes, hours, days, weeks and years. Time is the inevitable progression into the future with the passing of the present events into the past. Time waits for nobody; it's a quantity of duration. Time always moves, day and night. There's nothing that can stop time from flowing because time has its own ebb and flow. Many people have a lot of "why" questions caused by their lack of time management. Everything on earth is moving by time; even the death of people is controlled by time.

A person who does not respect time will always be the last person to organise things and to recognise the settlement of things. We often hear people saying, "time is money", "time is precious". Why do we say this? It's because all people know that time is what we need in order to survive in life.

Even studying is about time. When you study and move to the next grade according to your age, a lot of things go well. But when you fail and fail, then it becomes a problem because by the time you were supposed to be at university, you will still be in secondary school. Time is precious. When you were supposed to be working, you will still be in university.

Even in the Bible it's written that there's time for everything. (Ecclesiastes 3 verse 1) You can be tempted by things of this world because they happen before their true time comes. They happen because of the sin that Adam and Eve did from the beginning.

Check when adolescent and puberty stage start. It means your sexual hormones, cells and body are all ready for sexual intercourse. Even when they are ready, it does not mean it's time for you to sleep around with every boy or girl that you come across.

This moment of puberty and adolescent stage is an example of the push that makes people do things at the wrong time. This process makes people forget that everything has its own time. Because of how they feel many young people get themselves into sexual intercourse.

Here is a recommendation: Do you think that at your stage in life you can provide money for your baby? How are you going to take care of your baby? The reason for two to know each other as husband and wife is by the movement of time.

The right time for people to live as husband and wife is when they are done with their studies, because by then they will be able to get what they want without asking for money from their parents.

You get a wife or a husband when you are ready to be married. You are ready when you can be responsible to provide for yourself and to build your future with the money that you have worked for, not just the money that you've asked from someone.

A person more than 25 years old can stay alone if that person is not working, but a 21 year old person can have kids and a spouse when he or she is responsible for the family.

Here is an example. Many church members face this. A person receives a spiritual gift, maybe a gift of prophecy, teaching, evangelism, apostle, or pastoring. Within a month of receiving the gift, that person opens a ministry or starts to work. No, that is wrong; the timing is wrong. How do you start working without first learning how to use your gift? You must wait until the right, appointed time for you to work that comes eventually. Just receiving a gift does not mean you have the power or wisdom to lead; it means you are being marked as one of the heavenly workers or messengers. So, you must wait for the right time for you to work. Do not be tempted by things that happen as though it is their time to happen.

First check your position, yourself and your abilities, your strength, and your knowledge before you start doing things that use your gift. Respect time. It's important. Lack of time management disturbs a process of life. Time is precious.

Understanding Life

Dream and Vision

A dream is an imaginary event in the mind while sleeping, but I want to talk about a dream which consists of hope, goal, career, and hobby. They all fall under dreams that I want to discuss.

As different people we all have different gifts. A person does not choose a dream for another person. Even a parent does not have the right to choose a dream for his or her child.

A dream is something that suits a person. It is not what a person is forced to do or to choose, but we find people living under other people's dreams while they were supposed to be in their own dreams.

Your ability cannot be given to another person. People cannot change their abilities. What you dream is where your ability is and is where you will be living your own life.

Never choose a friend who tells you to follow him or her to his or her dream, but fight to reach yours. You have to do what is needed to feed your dream to have it come out. The dream your friend has is not the dream that you have. You might all be dreaming of becoming doctors but each of you is dreaming differently from one another. Never follow your friend's dream. Always follow what is needed in you to go to your dream.

I want to separate each letter of the word "dream" to provide points about your dream.

D-dedication

R-responsibility

E-effort

A-attitude

M-motive

If you have a dream it means you also have a vision, because a dream and a vision must be connected. Your dream must lead to your vision. A dream without a vision is doomed. If you say you are dreaming but you find yourself lacking dedication, responsibility, effort, attitude and motive, you are going nowhere. You must have them in order to go to your dream.

Until you add these characteristics, your dream will never become real. It does not matter what kind of dream you have, it's necessary that you have dedication, responsibility, effort, attitude and motive. Dream and take a step.

Understanding Life

Understanding Life

Seeking Saint but Finding Evil

I will never forget the time when I wanted to do good things, but found myself doing bad things. I wanted to do good things to my friend and I also wanted to do good things to God, but I found that I was doing the opposite of what I wanted to do.

The heading of this message says, seeking saint but finding evil. By this I mean:

- Seeking: to propose to want
- Saint: cleanliness or holiness and faithfulness
- But: opposite
- Finding: reach or getting
- Evil: wrongs, bad things, satanic

There was a time when I wanted to do good to my friend who goes by the name of Favoured, and there was also a time when I wanted to do good things to God. I got myself doing wrong things, not knowing why. I tried and tried to do good things to God and Favoured, but nothing worked for me.

I lived with pain inside of me, a pain caused by how life opposed me when I wanted to do good. I tried to do everything and to pray with care, and to speak with care, but nothing worked for me. All my ways were scattered.

There became a time when I did not know what to do about all these things. I asked myself 'What is it that opposes me when I want to do good things?' I got no answer, but I realized that lot of people are facing this challenge.

For me to solve this problem or this challenge was not easy. Even now this challenge sometimes awakens in my life, but I fight it day and night. It's too painful to love someone and never know how to show your love or care to that person.

This problem makes a lot of people end up stealing things so that they can make people they love happy. As people we need to give what we have, in order not to hurt other people or to steal people's property.

If you don't have what you want to give to your beloved one, just tell that person how much you love and feel about him or her. Tell him or her what you would like to do if you were able to do it. By doing so, you will be revealing things which are inside your heart and you will be giving yourself a relief.

Many people in a relationship find themselves lacking what they want to give to their partner. When they fail to get their desires, they end up stealing people's property so that they can give it to their beloved ones. As you propose to love with all your heart, you find yourself failing to give results of love.

There are many fruits of love which makes a person move from seeking saint but finding evil. This way of seeking saint but finding evil is when you steal people's property so you can give it to your beloved one.

The situation of seeking saint but finding evil happens mostly to couples. For me to solve mine, I spoke with God and Favoured, specifically telling them what and how I felt about them in my life. I was not in love with Favoured, but I was having a passion of caring much for her. I wanted to live for God with all my heart; even now I am fulfilling my desires on living for God.

I loved Favoured in a way that I wanted nothing wrong to happen to her, but all I wanted was to cherish her, to adore her, and to make her happy. For me to do this, I was supposed to be giving her money or something to show the care I have for her as a best friend amongst best friends.

There were times when I had no money and I had nothing to give to her. That emptiness broke my heart until I decided to tell her how I felt about her. To God it was hard because I hate doing evil, but evil was all over me. I loved God with all my heart and I prayed specifically telling God how I felt and what I could do if he could give me the chance to fight the evil trying to ruin me.

Let me tell you this: never stress when you want to do good things for someone, but you find out it's hard for you to do that thing. Just tell that person what you would do if you were able to do it or if you had money.

Never allow the bad to rule you. That is the only way to avoid stressing when you find yourself seeking saint but finding evil. It's too painful to care about someone and never know how you can let that person know or how you can show your love. This pain is the same as loving and not being loved in return. In both problems, you just wish you were able to open your heart to show someone how much you love and care about them. As you seek this way to show love and don't find it, it kills you inside.

This problem becomes more hectic when it comes to poor people who are treated as though they are useless because they don't have material or money to give to show care and love. Sometimes people reject you for no reason and when you ask why, the answer is 'You don't do anything. I am tired of you.'

Sometimes you find out that the person you thought will never leave you has stopped loving you. This is because many people are not happy by being loved only, but they want to do things even when they see that their money won't allow them. This is done by girls a lot. They want you to spoil them by taking them to places so that their friends can see them, but the truth will keep on being the truth. Keep on telling that person you love how much you love him or her. One day you might be understood.

Even when you aren't understood, you will find someone who will be the flesh of your flesh, bone of your bone, or who will understand you better. Keep on being honest and don't do evil so that you can get money to show love. Live the life you want. There's someone who will realize your love and care. Be strong.

Understanding Life

Understanding Life

Judgement is Everywhere

To judge someone is to tell them about things that they are doing that are right or wrong. When you judge, you often tell a person about his or her wrong activities and as you judge, you speak as though you don't do anything bad yourself. To advise or to judge are a little bit the same. The difference between judging and advising is how people pronounce or emphasize the words they say.

Advice is to tell someone what he or she must do to avoid trouble or to achieve something, but to judge is to tell a person about his or her wrongs in a way that implies that you do not do these wrongs and that he or she is the only person doing these wrongs.

Advice and judging can describe both the wrongs of a person and the goodness of a person. What makes these two things different is how people say the words when they are giving advice or judgement. The reason why the Bible says we must not judge and that God alone can judge is because when you judge it means you are a saint and nobody is a saint on earth. Even the preachers are not saints, but they are seen to be saints because of grace and their anointing.

We people are supposed to be advising not judging. Judging is for God alone. Because we don't know how to utter words properly, we end up judging instead of advising. We are full of judgement ways of speaking created by how we utter our words, but as you read here, I am sure you will learn your role as a person and you will also know God's role.

To advise is for a human. To judge is for God alone. Stay away from acting like a saint before people, but let us advise each other and admit that we all make mistakes and that some of us do evil things because of pressure. If you speak well, you will be doing a good work for God.

Tips of advice

There are lot of words that seem to be judging, but they are not judging, they are advice. Some examples are:

- Telling someone that he or she doesn't love himself or herself when that person sleeps around with a lot of people,
- Telling a person to stop drinking alcohol because he or she will die early,
- Telling someone that you can't marry her or him because that person did not take good care at himself or herself,
- Telling people to try to avoid sin.

Tips of judgement

There are lots of judgments which people make thinking they are advising and lots of advice that people make thinking they are judging. Examples of judgement are:

- To tell a person that that person is going to hell not heaven because you think that person sins a lot,
- To tell a person that that person will die as a prostitute with HIV and AIDS, because being a prostitute is not only about selling your body but also sleeping with many people with a ring in your finger,
- To ask a young preacher if he or she doesn't date and when you get the answer 'No' you say it's impossible.

We all have to learn how to utter words to people properly because how we speak counts a lot in people's life. How we speak can change the meaning of what we want to say even when we did not change the words.

Understanding Life

Understanding Life

Treatment Kills and Gives Life

The treatment I want to talk about is not medicine or tablets that we get in clinics and hospitals. I am talking about how we interact with people around us, how we live with them. In the whole world there is one weapon that can be used to show people love, care, respect and honouring. The weapon is treatment.

You can't tell a person that you love him or her but fail to treat that person well. Treatment has a positive way and a negative way. These ways affect people's life by leading to goodness or evil, life or death.

That is why we say 'Actions speak louder than words.' This saying is neutral, but the meaning of it comes from the word treatment. Actions are connected to treatment. It's impossible for someone to say 'I care for you' while actions, the treatment, do not show care. You can show a person that you love, care, and respect them without talking, but through treatment, your actions.

Some people are dying not because of illness or old age, but because of how they were treated. They died by over stress. A person can gain or lose strength because of the treatment from others. The most demolishing impact is from being treated badly by the ones next to your heart, the ones you are expecting to give you the best, the ones you think will never hurt you. Receiving bad treatment from these people hurts a lot.

We have to make sure that we treat each other in a good way, giving a treatment of love whenever we meet a person.

Many people are suffering. Some suffer because of how their parents treat them and how their friends, peers and neighbours treat them. Our treatment can ruin people's lives. If we fix our treatment of one another, we can change the world from evil to good. There are not many things which can make the world better, but if we change how we treat each other, we can move the world.

Understanding Life

Understanding Life

People Running People's Life

Parents

Parents rape their children; they don't support their children's dreams; they don't care about how their children grow. When they work far away, they don't call their children, they just call each other as parents, as husband and wife.

Children

Children, for much of the time, are careless about their parents. They insult their parents; they lie to their parents; they steal from their parents; they don't listen when their parents talk. They also kill their parents by stress.

Neighbours

Neighbours talk badly about you; they mock you as they make your life difficult. They can treat you as a stupid or take your wife or husband from you.

Teachers

Teachers tell learners that they are stupid, that they can't pass. They treat learners as useless people; they treat learners as if they hold the learner's life. Some sleep with learners, some choose learners to care for. Instead of paying more attention to people who don't understand anything at class, they pay more attention to those who have brains.

All the people mentioned above can change the world from evil to good. There are a lot of things which I did not mention when I explain about all those people, but the important thing is the bad treatment which causes the earth to be upside down.

If these people can change their bad treatment of other people, then the world will be free from death. Death is caused by a sin and if we treat each other badly it means we will face death in many ways.

- Why do you laugh at one another; don't you know it hurts to be laughed at.

- Why do you tell people that they are stupid while you know you can't allow to be told that to yourself.

Let us stop treating each other badly. Before you do something to another, think about putting yourself in that person's position. Then, if you know you would be hurt, don't continue hurting that person. Treating each other with care is a key to changing the world and to making us real humans.

Understanding Life

Understanding Life

Love and Lust

Love is something which can't be touched or seen, only felt. Love is defined in many ways, but to me love is an intense feeling of affection and care towards another person. Lust is a strong feeling of desire, especially of a sexual nature. It's a general want or longing, not necessarily sexual or devious.

A sexist is a person who discriminates on grounds of sexual lust, someone who practises sexism. Everyone wishes to be loved, but often we find that we were not loved. We were living under someone's lust or sexism.

Love is real and every person has love in himself or herself. Everyone is born with a heart to love, but the problem is how we show our love to others. In many ways, we make love seem not to exist because of the thoughts of people that produce lust or sexism. Love moves away and is under pressure.

Pillars of Love

- Caring
- Communication
- Faithfulness
- Trust

These things are the strong pillars of love. If a relationship lacks those things, it will not be able to survive.

Love is controlled by these things. Until they are there nothing will last. No matter what people do when they are together, love will not last without them. Love is not something which you choose to have for someone, but is something which is always active to connect to the right person. Love cannot be forced or chosen, but love can be created.

The things which create love are caring, communication, faithfulness and trust. If you give or show a person these things and find yourself living by these things, love is created. Even if you are friends who told one another that you want to be just friends, by the time those characteristics are produced in you, you will find yourselves in love with one another.

Be careful to conclude about love. Love does not rush for sex, but it rushes to care greatly for a partner. Many people lose their virginity so early because of concluding the things of love. When a person buys you something, it does not mean that person loves you. If that act of buying goes simultaneously with a person rushing to have sex with you, there's no love there. A person who loves you respects your privacy.

Many people are tempted by their lust, sexism and liking, but when you have feelings for someone it does not necessarily mean you love that person. Many have lost their womanhood because of following their feelings. Feelings will always lead people astray if they don't want to have a motive of loving someone.

If you want to follow your feelings, you will end up sleeping with different people even those who have diseases. But, love does not allow a person to sleep with lot of people. It resists because it's filled with care. Before you sleep with another person, think about your wife or husband. Then you will add faithfulness, care and trust. Feelings can be connected to any person because feelings come from sexist and lust, but love does not go there. A person that has love sees his or her lover as the best wife or husband in the whole world.

• A man with love sees his woman as the best woman and his eyes see his woman only.

- A woman with love sees her husband as the best and her eyes see no man apart from her husband.

- A man having feelings sees many women, but there's no care, faithfulness or truth. Everything will be about sex only.

- A woman with feelings sees many man, but there's no care, faithfulness or trust. Everything is about sex.

All people have sexist feelings, but when love begins, sexism stops being so important. Love begins and it gives fruits of care, trust and faithfulness. When you have feelings for someone, be careful of giving your body to that person, because no matter how your feelings are, it does not mean that the person loves you. You must realize how things fall apart because of love and sexist.

- Youth lose their virginity

- Parents sleep with their children

- Couples cheat

- Married people divorce

All these acts happen because of lust and sexism. If everyone can practise self-control, things will be well. We will see that those feelings we were thinking have perished.

Girls you need to wake up! Why do you misuse your bodies? You need to restore your womanhood, your value, and your dignity.

You cannot stop yourself from having feelings, but you can control them by being responsible for yourself. You are a precious creature that must be taken care of. A woman can be considered to be a fragile thing, but nowadays, women have forgotten their values, their dignity, and their womanhood. What they want is to satisfy their feelings by having sex with different people.

Many people leave people they love because of people they like. Why do you cheat for your wife or husband? You know you love your partner, but you cheat outside. By cheating you end up separating yourself from your beloved partner. Never leave the one you love because of the one you like. If you have a partner, never allow yourself to have another partner. Try to be faithful to your partner. Then you will see how awesome love can be to two people that love each other well. Love truly exists and love is true.

Love and sexist are natural. They will exist until God comes back.

Many girls get themselves into problems because they think they are getting a solution for their desires. Some sleep with celebrities expecting to be married in return. Some sleep with celebrities so they can tell people that they have slept with celebrity so and so. Many lose their virginity on celebrities. Girls are blinded by money. They forget that money is not life; money is not a healthy life.

Girls sleep with people they don't know because of money. They sleep with a person they are seeing for the first time and they don't know the status of that person. They treat celebrities as though they are not living on the same planet. What is wrong with women is because of poverty, lack of knowledge, lack of self-control, peer pressure, pride and being under the influence of alcohol or drugs. Some even sleep with a celebrity without using a condom so that they can tell friends that she has a child with a celebrity.

If that celebrity can allow himself to sleep with you, do you think he doesn't love to sleep with others? What was doing before he slept with you? Do you think he is a virgin celebrity? What if another person slept with him and give him HIV and AIDS? What if he is a player? Do you think he's a man who wants to marry a bitch? Do you think he can sleep with you while you know nothing about him and still want to marry you? No, no, no. It's obvious that he will think you are a bitch that loves sex.

What do you gain when you sleep with celebrities? I understand some women sleep with them because they are seeking a marriage, but that is not a good way of seeking a marriage to a celebrity. You would be better to give him or her a kiss and say that you don't play games with your body. If he is serious about you, he will make it happen at the right time. You don't have to make yourself a cheap person so that you can get in favour with celebrities. Girls, open your eyes. Know what you want in life and know what you must do in order to reach your desires.

Many women leave people they love because of the people they like. What I know is that love is strong and lasting, but lust is a momentary feeling. Hold on to the person that loves you. It's not easy to be loved. Don't be tempted by money. Money does not bring peace. The same celebrity you like can come home with another woman. What can you say because although you loved him, he did not come for you.

Your love is controlled by money. Many relationships that are controlled by money don't last long because a desire expires quickly. Do you think there are no girls that want to sleep with him the same way you slept with him? Do you think because he is with you he will not look for another woman?

Women, wake up! Don't seek money, but seek your right soulmate. Where there's a matching soulmate there's peace. Where there's no love, only lust operating, there's stress, problems and curiosity that causes anxiousness. It's time that as women you stand and speak as queens, even though you know that you are the one looking for love or a partner. Giving someone sex is not an approval of showing love. Don't make a mistake; he will leave you. Every man wants a woman with dignity, a woman who will be a good advertisement to people and the friends of that man.

He does not want a sex giver, but because a woman's mind is corrupted she thinks that giving sex is the only way of showing love. It is not the only way. A relationship that is controlled by money is weak and there's no love. True love can be found with a rich man or a poor man. It can't be maintained by money, but it stands for itself to give fruits of joy, peace, harmony and good life.

There's nothing that hurts more than a pain of love; even a pain of losing parents can't be compared with pain of love. Many people killed their parents only to stay with their lovers. You can even kill yourself for being rejected for no reason and later you find out there was another man or woman at your space. Jacob labored for fourteen years looking for a real and right woman.

A good woman must not be interested in a man's money or status, but she must seek loyalty, time, love and commitment. The problem with women is that they fall in love with playboys and then reject innocent boys that love them. Let your heart not be troubled; have self-direction in your life. Love is not in rich people, but love is everywhere. You can find the love that you deserve in a poor man. It happens that a poor man often has a greater love than a rich man.

Don't choose money, but choose the person with love. If you think that a rich man shows you love, then choose him. When a person doesn't have money, it seems that he or she doesn't have love. This is caused because women don't want to be loved; they want to see money that they can show to their families and friends. What I have found about women is that many women don't fall in love to be loved, but they fall in love expecting to gain. They don't concentrate on being loved, but they check what they want to gain.

They focus on money or good position of the husband, but they focus on gaining not love. This kind of mentality of women can destroy the world. Love is not a game. It's a weapon that has all the ability to do the complete good or bad things. Check yourself and know your position of dignity. Be a woman of value.

Love Yourself

Love has care in it. If you love yourself, you will care about yourself. Many people forget to love themselves, but they rush to love other people. They mostly love someone of the opposite gender. The bad part is that even when they love other people or their opposite gender, they still lack care that is needed in love. What we must know is that there's not lots of love, only one love. What happens is how we use this love because we can use it in different ways.

Love is used in relationships, families, friendship, and self-love. There's only one love that comes from God. That is the only love we must use. It has no hatred, anger, or betrayal, insults or any hurting thing or evil works. It always remains as love in bad and in good times.

Where there's love there is trust and faithfulness. True love has no pride, selfishness, hatred, grudges, care, hurts or self-centeredness.

This love I am talking about is the love that people use in doing lot of their things, but they don't use it well. There are good and bad parts of love. These parts of love can't be chosen and nobody knows which love he or she is facing, but as we begin to love, we all hope to be loved in return. Here are the good and bad parts of love;

Good Parts of Love

- you love and are loved in return
- you love and are appreciated and adored

69

- your partner makes you happy and refreshed

- you enjoy your childhood and adulthood

Bad Parts of Love

- you love and are not loved in return

- you love, but are used and insulted

- you are always in stress about your partner's actions

- you face lot of challenges; you can even kill yourself

There are lot of good and bad parts of love, but in all we must know what love is and how to use it.

How do we live our life when we are in love? Many people say that they love themselves, but you will find out that that person is having sex every day and they call that love.

Love is not about sex, but sharing of care, love, trust and harmony towards one another.

Until you know who you are, you will never be able to love yourself. Until you know your pride, dignity, goals, and responsibility, you will never know yourself.

If you sleep with any person of opposite gender, you are a person with no self-love. Taking the whole day without bathing your body or cleaning your mouth makes you a person with no self-love. Smoking, drinking alcohol, killing, insulting people, stealing, hurting people, holding grudges, not following the rules of life, all define a person with no self-love.

Self-Love

- respect for other people

- self-awareness
- pride
- dignity
- care
- peace
- healthy life
- order

Self-love is important in people's life. People with no self-love live as though they own everything, but people with self-love live with respect to everything. Self-love can make a person not hurt another person. When you love yourself, you will know what would happen to another person when some activities such as being used occur.

We should try by all means to have self-love. Check yourself and see what you can change in your life to create self-love in you. The rule of life is that before you love another person, love yourself. By doing that you will be able to treat another person the same way you treat yourself. If you love yourself, you will be able to love another person. The bible says, "Love one another as you love yourself." Self-love is the best.

Understanding Life

Solving Problems

A problem is a difficulty that has to be resolved or dealt with. It's a question to be answered which requires push and pull to solve. A problem is anything which is difficult to train or guide, anything unruly. A problem can change a person's life to a bad or good position.

There are different problems. Some problems push you to search for good future with all your heart; other problems put you under pressure in a way where nothing but death would solve the problem.

We don't choose the problems we have to face; they come without being called. For any problem there is a solution.

How to Solve a Problem

- identify the problem
- look at pros and cons
- Look at alternative decisions
- Communicate

By doing these things, you can solve your problems quickly. Many people lose lot of their values because of how they solve their problems.

Values

- respect
- education
- money
- family
- food

These values are ones that people can lose depending on how they respond to their problems. If you have a problem, do not spend all your time alone. Associate with people. They can help you forget your problem.

There are bad ways of solving problems which lead people to losing their values. The most important thing is how you respond to your problem. Today, those who face challenges of poverty respond in a bad way instead of responding in a good way. A good way is to study harder, but they decide to be killers, thieves or prostitutes.

Bad Ways of Solving Problems

- drinking alcohol
- joining gang or bad crew
- using drugs
- selling your body for money
- being a thief to get money
- smoking weed
- acting carelessly
- selling your soul to the devil to get money
- dropping out of school

There are lot of techniques that people use thinking that they are solving problems, while they are just creating other big problems. All the bad ways of solving problems have their own bad impacts. Those ways lead a person to end up with no good future, no healthy life. Many people end up in jail because of using those ways to solve their problems.

Stay away from solving your problems wrongly. Ninety percent of people use wrong ways to solve their problems and many end up in jail; some die early.

Use good ways to solve your problems. Those bad ways don't solve your problems. They may stop the problem temporarily, but to most people, the problem just gets worse. To show that those methods are bad, none of those ways lead to heaven. They are all against the will of God and the world.

As you finish using those bad ways, the problem remains. When you are sober minded, they come back. If you can use the good ways, your problems will go and never come back. Good ways lead to good things; bad ways lead to bad things. Recognise the types of ways you were using to solve your problem. In life we push and pull. Position yourself. Problems are natural; they won't be stopped. They will exist until we die.

Understanding Life

Getting Married at an Early Age

A marriage is a union of two or more people that creates a family tie and carries legal and social rights and responsibilities. A marriage is caused by love. The world is driven by love even the young people.

Getting married at an early age is often good, but sometimes it is bad. The world is filled with people who want to get married at an early age. The timing of when you get married has advantages and disadvantages. These are reasons why we get married early and why we get married late.

We must have a motive for a marriage. We must not get into a marriage before thinking of what it entails. Many people have gone into a marriage not because they were ready, but because they were afraid of losing the partners they have.

Some went into a marriage only to praise themselves that they are married.

There are many things which push people to get married at an early age before they are ready to be married. Many girls don't concentrate on their studies, but concentrate on finding a good husband. They concentrate on getting married at an early age and forget about building their future.

A good husband or a good wife is found not only by those who get married at an early age, but also those who get married when they are old. One thing that people forget, especially teenagers, is that we think we must fight for a marriage. That is wrong.

What belongs to you will always belong to you no matter what happens. The plans of God are not the plans of man. People are busy losing their virginity by sleeping with different people while trying to show love. Don't fight for love and don't fight to get a wife or a husband, but wait for the right time. The right time will always give you the best things.

The right time is when you are old enough to get married. This can't be when you are still at school or even in university. A marriage is something big and it needs a person who has taken his or her time to think carefully and has a motive for a marriage.

Advantages of Early Age Marriage

- you spend lot of time living in a marriage

- you get time to communicate with your children

- you face the future

- you own your life

- you eat what you want to eat

- you enjoy having all sexual activities at your age

- you get to understand the good and bad of the world

- you see yourself as an achieving person

- you face tough things and become strong to fight challenges

- you achieve lot of things by your drive

- you buy cars, house, etc, to make your family happy

Disadvantages of Early Age Marriage

- you need to know how to take care of your partner

- you jump from youth to a parent

- you have to work hard for the children
- you always face big challenges
- you'll always be scared of losing a marriage
- you stress about a lot of things
- you become sensitive
- you become dependent on a lot of people
- you face an early divorce
- you lack relationship knowledge
- you become a burden as a young person
- you lack money; you always spend for your family

Advantages of Being Single as a Young Person

- you spend your time alone, enjoying your youth
- you make your virginity, pride and dignity last
- you learn from others' mistakes
- your mind faces problems that you can solve easy
- you get help from many people who see you as a child
- you enjoy your time until you get tired of being alone
- you become dependent in a good way
- you get enough time to learn about relationships
- you get enough time to face your studies

- old people treat you as a good person because you don't rush to do things

Disadvantages of Being Single as a Young Person

- you are always lonely

- you lack relationship knowledge

- you masturbate because of lust

- you feel like you are a fool amongst other youth

- you are criticized often

- you think a lot, you stress

- you always feel shy to go near your peers' parties

- you are thought to be a fool; you won't get married

The good decision is to get married at a qualifying age and time. The right time and age should perhaps be at or above the age of 25 years.

Be careful of using your parents' money to get married if you don't work. What will you do and how are you going to survive if you don't have any money?

How are you going to survive on buying clothes, food, etc while you don't work?

Never be tempted; the right time will always be the right time the wrong time will always be the wrong time. There are things that display the right time and the wrong time in life. Before making a decision, check for those things. You will see the right time and follow the steps. The right time is always the best time.

Understanding Life

Understanding Life

Secrets in Families

A secret is anything that is hidden for people not to know. All families have their own secrets and their own shortcomings. The keeping of secrets can kill, but sometimes can bring protection. It does not matter what kind of family you have, rich or poor. The fact is that all families have their own secrets, but secrets in families are not all the same.

Different secrets

- secrets of why they are living

- secrets of why they are rich or poor

- secrets of parents or someone

- secrets of family curses

- secrets of ritual things

There are many secrets in families. Some of them are not mentioned here, but all families have secrets. Sometimes secrets that are held in families can kill a family if they are exposed. In most cases people fail to keep secrets from people they love, hence the exposure of that secret may turn to be poison in the life of the one that is told. If you love someone, you aren't supposed to keep secrets from that person, but it's not always the best plan. A personal life can't be exposed to people.

Many people have killed the people they love because by telling them what they were not supposed to know, they said wrong things and it didn't help.

Before you expose people's secrets, look for the results and acts that will appear after the news is out. Try to anticipate deeply before telling important secrets. Any person has a person to trust or to regard as the better one before all the friends or helpers.

If I tell deep secrets to the person I love, I must know that she has another person that she trusts, and that person has another one to trust. That is how secrets kill people. Never trust people by telling them secrets. Try by all means to hold it tight.

Some secrets can kill and some can heal hearts, but nobody knows which secret can kill or heal. When it's released, people forget about being sensitive and they rush on telling secrets before they know the outcomes of the news.

Never be overwhelmed by how a person treats you. You may speak about what you will regret. Learn to have self-control in everything you come across in life.

Here is an example of a person with a secret described in the Bible. Samson had a mighty secret that was supposed to be kept because God said so, but a person failed to keep what God said is a secret. Samson was overwhelmed by a woman and his love for a woman was why he told Delilah about his power.

Samson didn't know that by telling the secret to the person he loved could turn it into a poison in his life. After telling Delilah the secret, Samson lost many things, battles, his power, and his woman Delilah. What happened to Samson can also happen nowadays. Some of the secrets we tell turn against us after being released to people we love and trust. There is a time for some secrets to be known and there will never be time for some others to be known. Some of the secrets you have to take to the grave, but others you will tell when it's the right time.

Some exposes really help, such as telling someone the truth about his parents if he is not living with his biological parents. That will help that child accept anything that happens to him. Even when he is abused, he will know that 'these abusers are not my parents. I have to be strong

84

until I have my own property.' But when he doesn't know, he will be stressed a lot asking himself 'Why do my parents abuse me?'

Before Telling a Person's Secret, Consider

- will your secrets kill or give life

- will your secret bring peace or separation

- will your secret make you to gain or be in vain

- does the secret belong to you or another person

- why do you have that secret

- why is it a secret and not only news

- where did you get that secret

There are many questions to ask yourself before telling secrets. We know that people tell us secrets with a purpose. Some tell us because they trust that will keep the secrets safe. Some regard us as their best friend, but they didn't tell us. Some regard us as their helper, but they didn't tell us.

What we have to know is that we have been trusted with a secret and we have to do as we are expected to do. If you are living with a secret, ask yourself if the secret is yours or not. If it's not yours, tell it to the person whose secret it is, but if it's yours, fight to keep it with patience.

Let us learn to release and to keep secrets by the right time. Some people's future is hindered because of the secrets they don't know. If they knew, they would be free. Some people's failure is caused by the secrets they were told that they were not supposed to know. Take your time and do an introspection. Every person has a secret in his or her heart.

Understanding Life

To release it or keep it, the choice is yours, but time matters and determines the exposure moment.

Understanding Life

Understanding Life

People Are Not the Same

All people are not the same. Even twins are not the same although some are similar in complexion, body and face. Never treat another person in a way of repaying what another person has done to you. People are unique. It's time that we accept that people are not the same and we accept how every person lives.

Some people live a funny life, bad life, loving life, curiosity life, prayerful life, creative life, active life, respectful life etc., but all these people are unique. If there are two boys of the same age with the same complexion and height who also dress the same, it does not mean that they have the same mind. Two people will never have the same mind. What makes people to be so different is that they have different minds.

Even if two people got the same mark on a physics exam, the results are not the same. One got question 1 wrong, but the other one got it correct and got question 2 wrong.

We can't make people to be the same. God didn't create people to be clones. We can't be the same in our minds, desires, plays, and styles and the ways of doing things.

There was a woman whose child had a child friend next door. The woman's child was not gifted educationally and used to fail, while his friend next door was progressing normally. The mother of the child that failed would strike her son, asking him why he didn't progress as his friend next door did. Her child had no answer to the question. He just said 'I will progress, Mother. Please forgive me for crying.'

People are gifted in various things and they do things in a variety of ways. Accept the way a person is and learn to be considerate of all people. If your previous friend once promised you something and didn't fulfill the promise, it does not mean when your present friend promises you, he will also not fulfill his promises. People have variety of ways of doing things.

If your boyfriend slept with you and broke up with you afterwards, it does not mean all boys will break up with you after sex.

If a 25 year old man once raped or abused you, it does not mean that all 25 year old men will rape or abuse you and it does not mean that all 25 year old men rape or abuse people. It's time to accept that people are not the same.

We are afraid of accepting that people are not the same. Teachers know that learners are not all the same, but they still make other learners feel that they are useless if they don't get what other learners get. It's time for us all to appreciate everyone's effort and how each person is. Even God made people to be leading in different offices such as:

- politics
- school
- hospitals
- army
- dancing group
- acting group

If someone wants to choose a position for another person, that person might feel pressure because he did not choose what he was given. If your friend is a doctor, it does not mean you should also be a doctor. You decide based on your potential and limits.

Until we learn to accept that people are not the same, we will always judge people for how they live their lives. Live your life according to how you want to live it. Never chase the dream to be another person, even when you are inspired by his lifestyle, because each person's ability is different.

Understanding Life

Maturity

Maturity is the state of being ready or ripe. Maturity is an important factor in people's lives. It plays a big role on how a person lives his life and how he interacts with other people.

Maturity seems to be a gift, because many people want it, but don't have it. Maturity is something that you get from experiencing sadness and happiness, pains and miracles. Maturity is a key that leads to time management in people's lives.

Parents expect their teenagers to be mature on a certain time scale. There are different moments when maturity has to be seen. A person living without maturity always becomes a problem in other people's lives because he tends to do things without anticipating the outcomes.

A person with maturity always plans before acting. A mature person has his heart under control, but an immature person has a tendency to do things without considering other people. Maturity is needed as the key of life progress. The only way to live a harmonious life is when we have maturity; it allows us to live according to our strength and abilities.

When we talk about wisdom sometimes maturity is inside it. The reason why we go to schools and to any place where we learn about life is to get to be fed with words that give birth to maturity in our lives.

Maturity is similar to love, but people use it in different ways. If you love a person at one time and hate her another, it doesn't mean you don't have love. You just have a certain passion of feelings over that person. If a person is mature, that maturity works in everything from soccer to school.

Maturity in Variety of Things

- maturity in church

- maturity in school

- maturity in life in general

- maturity in leading people or living things

Maturity is used in different places. If a person needs maturity that person has to stick with people who have knowledge, wisdom, love, and maturity. There's a certain age when parents expect their children to be achieving some goals in their lives, but in most times parents are disappointed because children are not mature enough to do the expected things.

Some parents expect their male children to get a wife and a car at 25 years, but they are shocked when they see that their child is 27 years old and does not want a wife, a job or his own house. It's very disturbing for the parents when their 25 year old son doesn't want a wife and he fights to stay with his parents without going to work or doing something that will make money for the family.

In many times the maturity of a child is controlled by the environment in which a child is found. You will find a 25 year old person running outside class during lessons at school. Those acts are caused by lack of maturity. A person can fail until he becomes 25 years old by having good behaviour, but when he is found playing with children 15 years old when he should be in class, it shows lack of maturity.

Many people are being supported in their family home while not looking for work or a wife. They should understand that maturity comes with time. If a girl who is old enough to be married, is still running around chasing boyfriends instead of getting into a real courtship or relationship, that is a lack of maturity.

An immature person becomes a burden whereas a mature person always knows that by this time I have to hustle. I have to do this and this to move my life to a better place. Maturity comes from learning. If you need it, you have to be ready to learn, not only in school, but in everything that is part of life.

It also guides a person to a pure conscience. When you hear people saying that so and so is mature, it means that he has learned something. Maturity is knowledge put into actions.

The problem is that children who were supposed to be building their own families want to stay with their parents. It's time to check your age, do an analysis, and determine why you are like that at your age. Many people continue to act as youth and teenagers because they don't want to get a job to help their families or parents. Teens have to be led by their age when they want to do things. When choosing to be in a marriage, you have to be mature and ready.

Things that Show Lack of Maturity

- insulting your parents
- stealing for your parents
- being harsh or rising your voice over parents
- playing at school when too old to be at school

Things that Show Maturity

- respecting all old people
- being considerate
- having care over other people
- understanding all people the way they are

Things that Show Spiritual Maturity

- attending all the services

- being faithful

- avoiding what people say about you

- appreciating all a person does from his or her heart

- loving all people

- talking only good about other youth or people

Things that Show Lack of Spiritual Maturity

- gossiping church member

- lack of prayer over other people

- talking badly about other people

- attending church with time tables

- choosing another church when a time conflicts

- not being optimistic and patient

- poor lifestyle

Maturity is a gift from God, but maturity can be invited through learning and having experience. Fight to have it. It is a good director and peace maker.

DON'T BLAME PARENTS!!

Shalom!!!

Understanding Life

Understanding Life